PATHWAY BIBLE GUIDES

Alive with Christ

THE RESURRECTION

BY MATTHEW JENSEN

Alive with Christ
Pathway Bible Guides
© Matthias Media 2013

Matthias Media
(St Matthias Press Ltd ACN 067 558 365)
Email: info@matthiasmedia.com.au
Internet: www.matthiasmedia.com.au
Please visit our website for current postal and telephone contact information.

Matthias Media (USA)
Email: sales@matthiasmedia.com
Internet: www.matthiasmedia.com
Please visit our website for current postal and telephone contact information.

ISBN 978 1 922206 45 9

Cover design and typesetting by Matthias Media.
Series concept design by Lankshear Design.

CONTENTS

BEFORE YOU BEGIN

> If Christ has not been raised, your faith is futile and you are still in your sins. (1 Cor 15:17)

The resurrection of Jesus is at the very heart of the Christian faith. Without it, our faith is futile and we are still in our sins.

When asked about what they believe, most Christians would begin by explaining Jesus' death for sin and his resurrection. The apostle Paul's gospel message shows how central the resurrection is in the earliest proclamation of the gospel. His gospel message also includes a detailed list of eyewitnesses who saw Jesus after he was raised from the dead, clearly establishing the fact that Jesus was raised (1 Cor 15:5-8). For Paul, it was very important that Jesus was raised from the dead and that there were people who could testify to seeing him. In a world where there are many objections to Jesus' resurrection, we need to know this evidence and have confidence in the historical reliability of this fact.

Also, almost every speech in Acts by the apostles is about what the resurrection means and how important it is. The apostles taught that Jesus' resurrection changed the whole order of the world. The resurrection meant that God had finally acted to fulfil his promises to Israel (Acts 13:32-33).

But the resurrection of Jesus does not seem to be as earth-shattering for many people today. It can begin to seem like an ancient event with little relevance for us today. Even for Christians, the truth and importance of the resurrection can be lost.

These studies aim to bring us face-to-face with the resurrection. The studies are split into two parts. The first part looks at the eyewitness evidence for the resurrection of Jesus. The second part explores what Jesus' resurrection means for Christian living, hopes and certainty.

Each study in the first part investigates the resurrection appearances of Jesus found in one of the four gospels, building up a table of the appearances and eyewitnesses. In the appendices at the back of this booklet you will find some extra material on the evidence for the resurrection, a timeline for the empty tomb's discovery, and some extra material on Jesus' resurrection appearances.

After looking at the evidence for the resurrection, we will then move on to consider what the resurrection means for Christians today. For example, what does the resurrection tell us about who Jesus is, and about how we should respond to him? What is the relationship between Jesus' resurrection, our resurrection and the gift of the Spirit? How does the resurrection shape our lives?

My prayer is that these studies will give you great confidence that "in fact Christ has been raised from the dead", and that "in Christ shall all be made alive" (1 Cor 15:20, 22). May these truths shape your life in every way.

Matthew Jensen
October 2013

1. JESUS' RESURRECTION IN 1 CORINTHIANS AND MATTHEW

 **Getting started**

Why is Jesus' resurrection so important for Christianity?

If someone asked you what evidence there is for Jesus' resurrection, what would you say?

# Light from the Word

Read 1 Corinthians 15:3-8.

1. Fill in as much as you can of the following table about the eyewitnesses of the resurrected Jesus.

Verse	To whom did Jesus appear?
5a	
5b	
6	
7a	
7b	
8	

2. Why do you think Paul says that Jesus was raised "in accordance with the Scriptures"?

3. Why it is important that most of the five hundred brothers who had seen the risen Jesus were still alive (v. 6) when Paul wrote this letter?

4. How would you summarize the evidence for the resurrection in these verses?

Read Matthew 28:1-20.

5. Fill in the following table of eyewitnesses of the resurrected Jesus.

Verse	To whom did Jesus appear?	When did Jesus appear?	Where did Jesus appear?
9-10			
16-17			

6. What story did the chief priests and elders invent? Why is this
important?

 ## To finish

After looking at the evidence for Jesus' resurrection in 1 Corinthians
and Matthew, how would you answer the following objections to Jesus'
resurrection?

- The resurrection of Jesus from the dead is a hoax.

- The resurrection stories are legends.

- Jesus was not raised from the dead. The disciples just stole Jesus'
body.

 ## Give thanks and pray

- Thank God for the many eyewitnesses who saw the resurrected Jesus.
- Ask God to give you confidence in the resurrection of Jesus, and the
ability to explain the reasons for your confidence.

2. JESUS' RESURRECTION IN LUKE

 Getting started

From the previous study, how would you answer the following objection to Jesus' resurrection?

> Jesus was not raised from the dead. As the disciples thought about Jesus' death, they simply had a 'resurrection experience' because they came to understand that Jesus' death was the sacrifice for sin.

 # Light from the Word

Read Luke 24:1-53.

1. Fill in the following table of eyewitnesses of the resurrected Jesus.

Verse	To whom did Jesus appear?	When did Jesus appear?	Where did Jesus appear?
13, 18			
33-36			
34			
50-52			

2. Look back to the last study. What are the differences between the appearances of the risen Jesus in Matthew and Luke?

3. Who were the first eyewitnesses to the resurrection? Given that the testimony of women was rarely thought to be reliable in the ancient world (especially in courts of law), why do you think this detail of the story is significant?

4. In verses 25-27, 32 and 44-47, what does Jesus do to help Cleopas and his companion understand what has happened?

5. In verses 38-43, what evidence does Jesus offer to show that he has been physically raised from the dead?

 # To finish

After looking at the evidence for Jesus' resurrection in Luke, how would you answer the following objections to Jesus' resurrection?

- Jesus was not raised from the dead. He is still buried in the tomb.

- Jesus was not raised from the dead. His disciples only thought they saw him—it is a version of wishful thinking.

- Jesus' body was not raised from the dead. If anything happened it was a spiritual resurrection, not a physical resurrection.

 # Give thanks and pray

- Thank God for the many eyewitnesses who saw the resurrected Jesus.
- Ask God to give you confidence in the resurrection of Jesus, and the ability to explain the reasons for your confidence.

3. JESUS' RESURRECTION IN JOHN

 **Getting started**

How would you summarize the evidence we have seen for Jesus' resurrection so far?

From the previous studies, how would you answer the following objection to Jesus' resurrection?

> Jesus was not raised from the dead. The disciples sat down together and made up the whole story.

 # Light from the Word

Read John 20:1-21:14.

1. Fill in the following table of eyewitnesses of the resurrected Jesus.

Verse	To whom did Jesus appear?	When did Jesus appear?	Where did Jesus appear?
20:11-17	Mary Magdalene	Dawn of the 1st day of the week	outside the tomb
20:19	Disciples without Thomas	on the evening of the first Day	in a house with the doors locked.
20:26	Disciples with Thomas.	A week later in the house again.	in the house again with the doors locked.
21:2	Simon. Peter, Thomas Nathaniel Sons of Zebedee, James + John + two other disciples	Early in the morning	Jesus stood on the shore by the sea of Galilee

2. Look back at the previous study. What are the differences between the appearances of the risen Jesus in Luke and John?

3. What doubts does Thomas express? Why are these doubts understandable?

4. How does Jesus remove these doubts? How does Thomas respond?

To finish

After looking at the evidence for Jesus' resurrection in John, how would you answer the following objections to Jesus' resurrection?

- Jesus was not raised from the dead. The women just went to the wrong tomb. If they had gone to the right tomb they would have seen the body.

- Jesus was not raised from the dead. His disciples only thought they saw him—it is a version of wishful thinking.

- Jesus' body was not raised from the dead. If anything happened it was a spiritual resurrection, not a physical resurrection.

 ## Give thanks and pray

- Thank God for the many eyewitnesses who saw the resurrected Jesus.
- Ask God to give you confidence in the resurrection of Jesus, and the ability to explain the reasons for your confidence.

4. JESUS' RESURRECTION AND HIS LORDSHIP

 **Getting started**

We have now looked at the evidence in the Bible for the truth of Jesus' resurrection. We have seen the overwhelming evidence to confirm the fact that Jesus rose from the dead. What do you think this fact means for the identity of Jesus?

💡 Light from the Word

Read Matthew 28:16-20.

1. Now that Jesus has risen from the dead, what has he been given?

2. What response is called for?

Read Luke 24:44-49.

3. What does the risen Jesus say must happen immediately following his death and resurrection?

Read John 20:24-31.

4. How does Thomas respond when he meets the resurrected Jesus (v. 28)?

5. What do verses 30-31 tell us about why John wrote his gospel?

6. Why do you think this statement about why John wrote his gospel is placed immediately after his record of the resurrection appearances—particularly after Thomas' encounter with Jesus?

Read Acts 2:29-41.

7. We will return to Peter's sermon in Acts 2 in a later study. But for
    now, what are the main consequences of Jesus' resurrection? What
    does Peter urge the crowd to do in response to Jesus' resurrection?

 ## To finish

In this study we have looked at one of the basic consequences of Jesus'
resurrection: that as the risen Lord of all, he demands a response from
people everywhere. How would you summarize this response? How have
you responded personally to the risen Lord Jesus?

 ## Give thanks and pray

- Thank God for raising Jesus physically from the dead and giving him
  all authority in heaven and on earth. Thank God that Jesus is now the
  reigning Lord of the world, who gives forgiveness for sin.
- Ask God to help you respond to the risen Lord Jesus with faith and
  repentance.

5. JESUS' RESURRECTION AND OUR RESURRECTION

 **Getting started**

What do you think will happen to you when you die?

Light from the Word

Read 1 Corinthians 15:20-23.

1. Draw a timeline of the events described in this passage. How do these events give Christians confidence about life after death?

Read 1 Corinthians 15:42-49.

2. What are our bodies like now?

3. What will our resurrection bodies be like?

4. From both passages, when will we be given our resurrection bodies?

Read Ephesians 2:1-10.

5. What were we once like, and what is our situation now?

6. When and how did this change take place?

7. What does this passage say about what we should now use our bodies for?

 ## To finish

How should knowing that Jesus was raised change how you feel about death? How does knowing that believers are already raised spiritually change how you feel about death?

 ## Give thanks and pray

* Thank God for raising Jesus physically from the dead. Thank God that we can be confident of our future physical resurrection because Jesus was physically raised, and because we were spiritually raised when we first believed.
* Ask God to give you confidence in the face of death.

6. JESUS' RESURRECTION AND THE SPIRIT

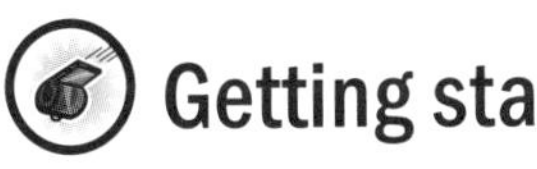 **Getting started**

What do you think the link is between the resurrection and the Holy Spirit?

☀ Light from the Word

Read Acts 2:22-39.

1. According to Peter, what are the key differences between Jesus and David?

2. Who exactly poured out the Holy Spirit at Pentecost? Why was he able to do this?

3. What is the main point of Peter's speech?

4. What is the link between the Spirit and forgiveness of sins?

Read Titus 3:3-8.

5. According to Paul, what were we like before we were saved?

6. How and why did God save us?

7. What is the result of our salvation?

 # To finish

As spiritually resurrected people, filled with the Holy Spirit, how should we live?

 # Give thanks, confess and pray

- Thank God that he raised Jesus from the dead and so has started the new age of the Spirit.
- Thank God that Jesus gives the Spirit to those who believe, with the result that we are saved, forgiven, and spiritually raised to devote ourselves to doing good works.
- Ask God to give you opportunities for living the good life of a Spirit-filled person, and ask him to help you to actively take up the many opportunities that he does provide.

7. LIVING THE RESURRECTED LIFE (I)

 **Getting started**

What do you hope for in life?

Read Romans 8:9-17.

1. List the results of having the Spirit (vv. 9-11).

2. What are the implications of having the Spirit (vv. 12-17)?

3. What is the identity of those with the Spirit (vv. 12-17)?

4. What does it mean to suffer with Christ and be glorified with him?

Read Romans 8:18-25.

5. Make a brief timeline of the events relating to 'the creation'. Where do we fit into this timeline?

6. What are we waiting for?

 # To finish

Complete the following quotes from Romans 8:9-25:

The body is ___________________________________ (v. 10)

The spirit is ___________________________________ (v. 10)

He who raised Christ Jesus from the dead will also ___________

___________________________________ (v. 11)

If children, then ___________________________________

___________________________________ (v. 17)

We wait eagerly for our adoption as sons, ___________________

___________________________________ (v. 23)

How must these great realities shape what we hope for?

 # Give thanks and pray

- Thank God for the gift of his Spirit who gives spiritual life to our bodies, enables us to call God 'Father', and unites us to the sufferings and glories of Jesus.
- Ask God to help you live according to the Spirit and not the flesh as you wait eagerly for the physical resurrection.

8. LIVING THE RESURRECTED LIFE (II)

Getting started

In the last study we saw that the Spirit gives life to our mortal bodies (Rom 8:11). What do you think this looks like in the life of the believer?

☀ Light from the Word

Read Romans 6:8-14.

1. How must we 'consider ourselves' because of Christ and his resurrection?

2. How then should we be living and using our bodies?

Read Romans 12:1-2.

3. What are the commands in these verses?

4. How do the commands (and the reasons for them) follow from what we have already seen in Romans about Jesus and his resurrection?

Read Romans 12:3-21.

5. What do these verses say about being part of the "one body in Christ" (v. 5)?

6. In a few words, how would you summarize the Spirit-filled life of being a "living sacrifice" (v. 1), as spelled out in these verses?

 **To finish**

What part do you play in the body? How can you play your part for the benefit of the rest of the body?

List one command in these verses that:

- you find (relatively) easy to keep

- you particularly struggle to keep

- you had never noticed in the Bible

 ## Give thanks and pray

- Thank God for Jesus' resurrection. Give thanks that it starts the new age in which he gives us his Spirit, who gives life to our mortal bodies so we can live as his servants.
- If you're in a small group, pray with someone else in your group about:
    - your church and how its members use their gifts (from 12:3-8)
    - how you exercise your gifts at church
    - a command you particularly struggle to keep (from 12:9-21).

APPENDIX (I): EVIDENCE FOR JESUS' RESURRECTION

There are two main strands of evidence for Jesus' resurrection.

First, there is the evidence of the empty tomb. This is the forensic evidence; the evidence at the 'crime scene' that indicates that something did happen because Jesus' body was no longer in the tomb. All four gospels record that the tomb did not contain Jesus' body on the Sunday morning. At least six people (Mary Magdalene, Mary the mother of James, Salome, Joanna, Simon Peter and John) went to the tomb and saw that Jesus' body was no longer in it. Matthew even notes that the Jews of Jesus' day acknowledged the tomb was empty, since they needed to come up with an explanation for it (i.e. that the disciples stole the body, as recorded in Matt 28:12-13). The tomb contained Jesus' grave clothes lying where Jesus had been laid, but no body. From this strand of evidence, it is obvious that something happened. However, the most that can be said with certainty is that the body of Jesus was no longer in the tomb. This evidence does not suggest what exactly happened to the body. For the answers to these questions, we need to look at the second main strand of evidence.

This is found in the testimonies of the eyewitnesses to the resurrection of Jesus. The gospels record the fact that after his death, Jesus appeared alive to a number of his followers. This was in fulfilment of Jesus' own predictions (see, for instance, Luke 9:22 or John 2:18-22)—predictions that his followers did not understand at the time. Jesus appeared in many different locations to many different people at many different times. He ate and drank with his followers and explained to them why he had come back to life. It's important to note that these eyewitness testimonies come from people who previously were not expecting Jesus to rise from the dead. And some of the eyewitnesses later died for their belief in the resurrection (one of them—Saul/Paul—after being transformed from a persecutor of the church to one of its greatest missionaries). This second strand of evidence is more like the testimonies of witnesses in a court case, where witnesses testify to what they have seen and heard. In this case, the witnesses include some unlikely people (i.e. women—regarded as unreliable witnesses in the world of the first century—and uneducated fishermen) but this does not disqualify their testimony. In fact, it suggests even more strongly that the evidence is true, as these stories are unlikely to have been invented. The one well-educated and significant witness by the world's standards (Paul) uses this second strand of eyewitness evidence to argue for the resurrection. He wrote that Jesus appeared to more than 500 people at one time and that most of them were still alive at the time that Paul wrote, and so their testimonies could be checked against each other and against the written records.

So then, these two strands of evidence work together to explain that Jesus rose from the dead. The first strand is crucial as it shows what happened at the 'crime scene': Jesus' body was no longer in the tomb. The second strand shows us that the evidence is far greater than just the empty tomb: it includes eyewitness testimonies of people who saw Jesus after he had died—people who testified to walking, talking, eating and speaking with the risen Jesus.

APPENDIX (II): A TIMELINE FOR THE EMPTY TOMB'S DISCOVERY

There is one common objection to Jesus' resurrection that we have not covered in these studies: the objection that the gospel accounts of the resurrection conflict with each other and therefore should be ignored as evidence.

We have read about the discovery of Jesus' empty tomb, and about the accounts in Matthew, Luke and John of his resurrection appearances, with each gospel recording different details of these events. The discovery of the empty tomb is recorded in all four gospels, while the resurrection appearances are different in each gospel. In each gospel, Jesus appears to different people. This means there are two possible types of conflict: first, the details in each description of the discovery of the tomb appear to be different; and second, different people are said to have met the risen Jesus.

It is not difficult to explain the fact that different authors recorded Jesus meeting different people after his resurrection. They did not record every instance of the risen Jesus meeting someone, but only those meetings that were passed on to them by their eyewitnesses or that fit their particular purposes and emphases. It is also not difficult to develop a timeline of Jesus' appearances and where these took place. You could read back through the tables of witnesses that you have put together over the first three studies and do this for yourself. We have also included a suggested list in appendix (iii). So the objection of conflict in this area is shown to be weak.

However, it is more difficult to put the passages about the discovery of the empty tomb into the same sort of order. This is because each of the gospels seems to record the same event, but in each description there are apparent differences. However, on close inspection, the various accounts harmonize without any contradiction. You might like to sit down and try to harmonize the four accounts for yourself, but as an aid to this task, you might also like to read through the suggestion below and compare it with the information recorded in the four gospels.[1]

Passage	What happened
Matthew 28:2-4	Before dawn (but after the actual resurrection), an earthquake occurs, an angel rolls the stone away from the entrance to the tomb, and the guards flee.
Matthew 28:1 Mark 16:1-4 John 20:1	After sunrise, Mary Magdalene, Mary the mother of James, and Salome approach the tomb but discover the stone rolled away. They enter the empty tomb.
John 20:2	Mary Magdalene immediately leaves the tomb to tell Peter and John that Jesus' body is gone.
Matthew 28:5-8 Mark 16:5-8	Inside the tomb, Salome and Mary the mother of James see an angel (described in Mark 16:5 as a young man), who announces the resurrection. The women return to the city, but are in such awe that they are left temporarily speechless.
Luke 24:1-9	A group of women from Galilee (cf. Luke 8:3 and 23:55) arrive at the tomb to anoint Jesus' body. They meet two men (later described as angels in Luke 24:23), then return to report the message of the resurrection "to the eleven and to all the rest" who have now reassembled (cf. Matt 26:56).

Luke 24:12 John 20:3-10	Meanwhile, after hearing from Mary Magdalene, Peter and John (perhaps joined by others; cf. Luke 24:24) run to the tomb, see the grave clothes, and return home.
John 20:11-18	Mary Magdalene follows Peter and John to the tomb, sees two angels, and then meets the risen Jesus. She returns to inform the disciples that Jesus has risen.
Matthew 28:9-10 Luke 24:10-11	Mary the mother of James and Salome meet Jesus and are told to instruct Jesus' "brothers" to go to Galilee, where he will meet them. Despite having now received numerous reports about the empty tomb and the resurrection, the disciples do not yet believe these reports.

1. For more information see Murray Harris, *Raised Immortal: Resurrection and Immortality in the New Testament*, Marshall, Morgan and Scott, London, 1983, pp. 69-70.

APPENDIX (III): JESUS' RESURRECTION APPEARANCES

From the passages that record the resurrection appearances of Jesus, it seems that Jesus appeared to people a total of 12 times after his resurrection. If we follow the order of events outlined in appendix (ii), the appearances of Jesus would be as follows:

Passage	To whom did Jesus appear?	When did Jesus appear?	Where did Jesus appear?
John 20:11-17	Mary Magdalene	Dawn, the first day of the week	At the tomb
Matthew 28:9-10	Mary the mother of James, and Salome	The morning of the first day of the week	Going from the tomb to the disciples
Luke 24:34 1 Corinthians 15:5	Simon (Peter)[1]		
Luke 24:13, 18	Cleopas and another disciple	On the third day, in the afternoon/ evening	On the road to Emmaus, and at Emmaus
Luke 24:33-36 John 20:19	The eleven and others, including Cleopas (Thomas absent)	On the third day, at night	In Jerusalem

John 20:26 1 Corinthians 15:5	The twelve (Thomas included)	After eight days	In Jerusalem
John 21:2	Peter, Thomas, Nathanael, the sons of Zebedee, two others	At dawn	At the Sea of Tiberias
Matthew 28:16	The eleven		In Galilee on a mountain
1 Corinthians 15:6	More than 500		
1 Corinthians 15:7	James		
Luke 24:50-52 Acts 1:3-12 1 Corinthians 15:7	All the apostles	40 days after the resurrection	Mount of Olives
Acts 9:3-17, 22:6-7, 26:13-14 1 Corinthians 15:8	Saul/Paul	At noon	Approaching Damascus

1. cf. John 1:42

FOR THE LEADER

What are Pathway Bible Guides?

The Pathway Bible Guides aim to provide simple, straightforward Bible study material for:

- Christians who are new to studying the Bible (perhaps because they've been recently converted or because they have joined a Bible study group for the first time)
- Christians who find other studies[1] too much of a stretch.

Accordingly, we've designed the studies to be short, straightforward and easy to use, with a simple vocabulary. At the same time, we've tried to do justice to the passages being studied, and to model good Bible-reading principles. We've tried to be simple without being simplistic; no-nonsense without being no-content.

The questions and answers assume a small group context, but it should be easy to adapt them to suit different situations, such as individual study and one-to-one.

Your role as leader

Because many in your group may not be used to reading and discussing a Bible passage in a group context, a greater level of responsibility will fall to you as the leader of the discussions. There are the usual responsibilities of preparation, prayer and managing group dynamics. In addition, there will be an extra dimension of forming and encouraging good Bible reading habits in people who may not have much of an idea of what those habits look like.

Questions have been kept deliberately brief and simple. For this reason, you may have to fill in some of the gaps that may have been addressed in, say, an Interactive Bible Study. Such 'filling in' may take the form of asking follow-up questions, or using your best judgement to work out when you might need to supply background information. That sort of information, and some suggestions about other questions you could ask, may be found in the following leader's notes. In addition, a *New Bible Dictionary* is always a useful aid to preparation, and simple commentaries such as those in the *Tyndale* or *Bible Speaks Today* series are often helpful. Consult these resources after you have done your own preparation.

On the question of background information, these studies are written from the assumption that God's word stands alone. God works through his Holy Spirit and the leaders he has gifted—such as you—to make his meaning clear. Assuming this to be true, the best interpreter and provider of background information for Scripture will not be academic historical research, but Scripture itself. Extra historical information may be useful for the purpose of illustration, but it is unnecessary for understanding and applying what God says to us.

The format of the studies

The discussion questions on each passage follow a simple pattern. There is a question at the beginning of each discussion that is intended to get people talking around the issues raised by the passage, and to give you some idea of how people are thinking. If the group turns out to be confident, motivated and comfortable with each other and the task at hand, you may even decide to skip this question. Alternatively, if the group members are shy or quiet, you may decide to think of related types of questions that you could add in to the study, so as to maintain momentum in a non-threatening way.

After the first question, the remaining questions work through the passage sequentially, alternating between observation, interpretation and application in a way that will become obvious when you do your own preparation. The final question of each discussion, just before the opportunity for prayer, could be used in some groups to encourage (say) one person each week to give a short talk (it could be 1 minute or 5 minutes, depending on the topic and the people). The thinking here is that there's no better way to encourage understanding of a passage than to get people to the point where they can explain it to others. Use your judgement in making the best use of this final exercise each week, depending on the people in your group.

In an average group, it should be possible to work through the study in approximately 45 minutes. But it's important that you work out what your group is capable of, given the time available, and make adjustments accordingly. Work out in advance which questions or sub-points can be omitted if time is short. And have a few supplementary questions or discussion starters up your sleeve if your group is dealing with the material quickly and hungering for more. Each group is different. It's your job as leader to use the printed material as 'Bible Guides', and not as a set of questions that you must rigidly stick to regardless of your circumstances.

Preparation: 60/40/20

Ideally, group members should spend half an hour reading over the passage and pencilling in some answers *before* they come to the group. Not every group member will do this, of course, but encourage them with the idea that the more they prepare for the study, the more they will get out of the discussion.

In terms of your own preparation as leader, we recommend you put aside approximately *two hours*, either all at once or in two one-hour blocks, and that you divide up the time as follows:

- 60 minutes reading the passage and answering the questions yourself as best you can (without looking at the leader's notes or Bible commentaries)
- 40 minutes consulting the leader's notes (plus other resources, like commentaries). Add to your own answers, and jot down supplementary questions or other information that you want to have available as you lead the discussion. Make sure you write everything you need on the study pages—the last thing you want to do is to keep turning to the 'answers' in the back during the group discussion
- 20 minutes praying about the study and for your group members.

This 60/40/20 pattern will help you to focus on the Bible and what it's saying, rather than simply regurgitating to the group what is in the leader's notes. Remember, these notes are just that—notes to offer some help and guidance. They are not the Bible! As a pattern of preparation, 60/40/20 also helps you to keep praying for yourself and your group, that God would give spiritual growth as his word is sown in your hearts (see Luke 8:4-15; 1 Cor 3:5-7).

If, for some reason, you have less or more time to spend in preparation, simply apply the 60/40/20 proportions accordingly.

---

1. Such as the Interactive Bible Study (IBS) series also available from Matthias Media.

1. JESUS' RESURRECTION IN 1 CORINTHIANS AND MATTHEW

▶ **Remember 60/40/20**

 ## Getting started

The opening question is designed to show people that they may be someone who acknowledges the importance of the resurrection without having thought through the reasons for its importance. The aim is to give motivation for the whole set of studies, as this is the exact issue the studies are discussing. You may like to point people back to the introductory comments in this regard.

The second question introduces the task that each of the first three studies asks us to complete in the 'To finish' section. We need to be able to answer other people's objections (and our own doubts) about the resurrection. As we consider the evidence, it is important that this is not just an exercise in history, but one that gives us confidence and allows us to be better evangelists (cf: 1 Pet 3:15).

Studying the passage

The main aim of this section is to get people to read through 1 Corinthians 15:3-8 and Matthew 28:1-20, where they will begin to see the rich evidence for Jesus' resurrection. The tables are designed to help in this task, although it should be noted that there is evidence outside the categories used in these tables. You might like to read through (or direct people's attention to) appendix (i), because it discusses the types of evidence that we can find in these passages. So in Matthew 28 there is further evidence such as the tomb being empty, the guards' witness to the Jewish authorities, and the explanation of the origin of the view that Jesus' body was stolen by his disciples.

You will not be able to fill in all the boxes on the charts. They are included so that people can synthesize the material later, if they wish. One of the many possible ways to put this all together is by reading appendix (iii), which lists all of Jesus' post-resurrection appearances—but do not yet direct people to this extra material, as it will take away their opportunity to discover it for themselves from the texts.

After completing the first table, you should end up with something like this:

Verse	To whom did Jesus appear?
5a	Peter
5b	The twelve
6	More than 500
7a	James
7b	All the apostles
8	Saul/Paul

The following questions help us to look closely at various details from the passage. Paul's use of the phrase "in accordance with the Scriptures" reminds us that Jesus' death and resurrection fulfilled numerous Old Testament prophecies pointing to these great events. The reference to 500 eyewitnesses—most of whom were still alive—provides powerful evidence that the resurrection really happened. Paul is inviting his readers to seek out these witnesses and hear their testimony, which means that the story of the resurrection could never have survived if it was an invention.

Verse	To whom did Jesus appear?	When did Jesus appear?	Where did Jesus appear?
9-10	Mary the mother of James, and Salome	The morning of the first day of the week	Going from the tomb to the disciples
16-17	The eleven		In Galilee on a mountain

One of the possible difficulties that people may experience when synthesizing this material involves the way the dates are recorded. The dating difference between the third day (1 Cor 15:4) and the first day (Matt 28:1) is due to the way time is reckoned. In 1 Corinthians, it is the number of days (or part-days) from the time Jesus died. In Matthew, it is related to the start of the week. So there is no contradiction; these are simply different ways of expressing the same period of time.

 # To finish

This closing section aims to help people answer their own doubts and questions. It is good to acknowledge that people do have doubts in this area, and that we are trying to help people gain confidence for themselves as much as to work out answers to common objections.

To the objection that Jesus' resurrection is a hoax, the simplest answer is to note that the tomb was empty and that there were many different eyewitnesses, so something must have happened to the body.

To the objection that the resurrection stories are legends, note that these 'legends' have historical eyewitness testimony—not just from individuals but also from entire groups of people who saw Jesus. As we saw above, even in Paul's day, there were lots of people who saw Jesus and were able to be asked.

To the objection that the disciples stole the body, Matthew's Gospel clearly shows that the authorities of Jesus' time suspected the disciples may attempt some kind of theft, so they placed guards on the tomb to prevent this (cf. Matt 27:62-66). The presence of these security guards means that it was not possible for a theft to have happened. Further, this objection has its roots in the Jewish authorities of Jesus' time, so is nothing new.

 # Give thanks and pray

Depending on the maturity level of those in your group, you may also wish to make a list of people to pray for, especially that God would give you opportunities to speak to them about the resurrection.

2. JESUS' RESURRECTION IN LUKE

▶ **Remember 60/40/20**

 ## Getting started

This opening question aims to get you back into not only the previous study's material but also the task of using the historical evidence from the biblical texts to answer people's objections. In answering this objection, two things should be noted: first, the objection has as its starting point the assumption that the resurrection did not happen; second, it is trying to explain the phenomenon experienced by the disciples while denying the disciples' own explanation.

Studying the passage

The completed table should look something like this:

Verse	To whom did Jesus appear?	When did Jesus appear?	Where did Jesus appear?
13, 18	Cleopas and another disciple	On the third day, in the afternoon/evening	On the road to Emmaus, and at Emmaus
33-36	The eleven and others, including Cleopas	On the third day at night	In Jerusalem
34	Simon (Peter)[1]		
50-52	All the apostles	40 days after the resurrection	In the vicinity of Bethany

The subsequent questions focus our attention on some of the details of the passage. Taken together, they reinforce the historical reliability of Luke's account (as it's highly unlikely a first-century story would have been invented in which women were crucial eyewitnesses), the centrality of the Scriptures in understanding Jesus' resurrection (as this is where Jesus turns to open the eyes of his companions on the road to Emmaus), and the reality of Jesus' bodily resurrection (as he eats with his disciples).

The final question in this section aims to prompt people to begin the task of synthesizing the evidence presented in the gospels. It reviews the material from the last study and asks them to see that we have lots of information—information that is not mutually contradictory but rather is supportive of the resurrection. One way to synthesize the material from all three studies in this first section is by reading appendix (ii), which outlines a timeline for the empty tomb's discovery. It is worth pointing people to this extra material if they are concerned or worried, but it is best not to read it until after you have finished the first three studies, as it may spoil study 3 on John's Gospel.

 # To finish

Again, three objections to the resurrection are listed for the group to consider and to answer. These should help people with their concerns but also ready them to provide an answer to others. The question asks people to use Luke to answer the objections (though it does not matter if they also use 1 Corinthians and Matthew).

To the objection that Jesus is still buried in the tomb, the answer should involve the observation that the tomb was empty, and that Jesus appeared to his disciples multiple times in different places.

To the objection that the disciples only thought that they saw Jesus or that Jesus was not raised physically because it was only a spiritual resurrection, it should be pointed out that in addition to the multiple witnesses who saw Jesus, some also touched him and ate with him. He was physically raised and was seen up close by multiple eyewitnesses. This could not simply have been a spiritual experience, or wishful thinking.

 # Give thanks and pray

If you made a list at the end of study 1 of people to pray for, go back to that list and pray for the same people again, especially that God would give you opportunities to speak to them about the resurrection.

---

1. cf. John 1:42

3. JESUS' RESURRECTION IN JOHN

▶ Remember 60/40/20

 ## Getting started

The opening questions are again aimed at reminding people where we have come from in these studies. There are different types of evidence for the resurrection—in particular, the empty tomb and eyewitnesses. We have seen both types in various levels of detail. It is worth briefly looking back over the past two studies (especially the tables) to refresh people's minds. This also allows people to think about how they would answer the objection that the disciples invented the whole thing. The historical evidence (both the empty tomb and eyewitnesses to the resurrected Jesus) is overwhelming. Additionally, many of the disciples died for the sake of this 'invented story', indicating that it was not made up. Do people really die for the sake of protecting stories they know they have invented?

Studying the passage

The completed table should look something like this:

Verse	To whom did Jesus appear?	When did Jesus appear?	Where did Jesus appear?
20:11-17	Mary Magdalene	Dawn, the first day of the week	At the tomb
20:19	The eleven and others (Thomas absent—John 20:24)	On the third day, at night	In Jerusalem

20:26	The twelve	On the eighth day	In Jerusalem
21:2	Peter, Thomas, Nathanael, the sons of Zebedee, two others	At dawn	At the Sea of Tiberias

The questions about Thomas are intended to help us sympathize with his doubts, and more importantly to show that Jesus was willing and able to remove these doubts—resulting in Thomas' great declaration of Jesus being his Lord and his God (v. 28). It is both a powerful testimony about the identity of the risen Jesus ("my *Lord* and my *God*"), and a very personal declaration of how Thomas now relates to Jesus ("*my* Lord and *my* God").

The final question in this section aims to prompt people to go further in synthesizing the evidence in the gospels. It reviews the material from study 2 and helps them to notice that we have a wealth of information that is supportive of the resurrection. As mentioned previously, one way to synthesize the material from all three studies in this first section is by reading the material in appendix (ii). Now would be a good time to point people to this extra material if they have not yet read it.

# To finish

Again, three objections to the resurrection are listed for the group to consider. Two of them are the same as those seen in the last study, demonstrating that there is double the amount of evidence to answer the objection compared to what we saw last time. Only the first objection (suggesting that the women went to the wrong tomb) is new. In answer to this objection, it is worth nothing that this scenario requires both Peter and the beloved disciple (John) to have gone to the wrong tomb (in addition to the women). Further, Matthew 27:61 and Luke 23:55 record that the women knew exactly where Jesus was laid.

# Give thanks and pray

If you made a list in study 1 of people to pray for, then pray again that God would give you opportunities to speak to them about the resurrection, and that he would show mercy and open their eyes.

4. JESUS' RESURRECTION AND HIS LORDSHIP

▶ Remember 60/40/20

 ## Getting started

This opening question aims to move you from thinking about the historical evidence examined in the first three studies to thinking about the consequences of Jesus' resurrection for Christian living. There will be a number of different answers given throughout the remaining studies (confidence in the face of death, the gift of the Spirit, a basis for ethical living), but this study focuses on perhaps the most basic result: that Jesus is now the Lord of heaven and earth. Knowledge of Jesus' lordship should result in our repentance and submission to him as Lord.

Studying the passage

This section asks you to re-read part of the resurrection narratives from Matthew, Luke and John in order to see that each recounts not only the historical evidence for Jesus' resurrection, but also its significance. In particular, we will focus on the idea of responding to the risen Lord Jesus with repentance, faith and obedience.

Matthew 28:16-20 records Jesus' announcement that all authority in heaven and earth has now been given to him (v. 18). The consequence of this is that all people everywhere ("all nations") should become his disciples and be taught to obey all that he has commanded. You may also like to mention the enormous comfort of knowing that the Lord of the universe is with us as we go about the task of making disciples (v. 20), but our primary focus is on the initial response of turning back to Jesus as Lord and following him.

Luke 24 explains the significance of the death and resurrection of Jesus in terms of repentance and forgiveness of sin (v. 47). As we turn back (i.e. repent) and submit to the risen Jesus, we are placing ourselves under the lordship of the one who has authority and power to forgive our sins, having died for us and been raised to life.

In John 20, Thomas meets the risen Jesus and confesses that Jesus is his 'Lord' and his 'God' (v. 28). Thomas repents of his unbelief and submits himself completely to Jesus. John then immediately moves on to explain his purpose in writing his gospel: to demonstrate that Jesus is the Christ, the Son of God, in order that his readers might have life in Jesus' name (v. 31). The fact that this statement is placed immediately after the climactic event of Thomas' encounter with Jesus is enormously significant. It indicates that the resurrection is the key event (the greatest 'sign' recorded by John) that proves Jesus is the Christ, and the one who can offer life. Here again, we can use the key concept of repentance to understand the right response to the risen Jesus. Recognizing that Jesus is Lord, God, and Christ will involve turning from other gods and other beliefs, bowing the knee to Jesus and submitting to him—that is, it involves our repentance.

Finally, in Acts 2 we read a clear summary of the apostles' preaching, in which the consequences of Jesus' resurrection are clearly explained as repentance and forgiveness. God has overturned the human verdict on Jesus (i.e. crucifixion—see verses 23-24 and 36), and has made Jesus "both Lord and Christ" and exalted him to his right hand. The only appropriate response is to turn back to Jesus and submit ourselves completely to him.

In summary, Jesus' resurrection means he now has all authority and power—he is the promised Christ, the risen and exalted Lord of all—and so our response should be one of repentance.

Throughout this study, it will be important to help people see that repentance is not simply a one-time response when we first become Christian (although this is vital). Rather, ongoing repentance will characterize the Christian life as we bring every part of our existence, big and small, under the lordship of the crucified and risen Jesus.

 # To finish

This final question asks people to think about how they have changed in light of the knowledge that Jesus is Lord. This is a good opportunity to hear some people's testimonies and to explain how you came to faith, but it also should be used to get people thinking about their ongoing Christian walk. Are they living under Jesus' lordship? In what areas of life do they still need to repent? The final two studies will return to the idea of living the resurrected life with Jesus as Lord.

5. JESUS' RESURRECTION AND OUR RESURRECTION

▶ **Remember 60/40/20**

 ## Getting started

As we continue with the second stage of our studies, the aim is to make the significance of the historical reality of the resurrection clear for people's thinking, feelings and hopes. The opening question will elicit responses in all three of these categories. Some people will have wrong views of death, which will be corrected by the end of the study. Others will be upset at thinking about death, or will feel scared of death. By the end of this study, people should no longer hold the same fear of death, because they should see the certainty of our hope for the future as we think about the resurrection.

Studying the passage

The following questions each lay down a plank in an argument that is drawn together in the questions that finish the study. The argument is this: because Jesus was raised physically from the dead (a point we have established in the first three studies), we can be confident of our physical resurrection when he returns. More than that, because Jesus was raised we also were spiritually raised when we believed the gospel of the resurrection.

So 1 Corinthians 15 links our resurrection to Jesus' resurrection: Christ first, and then us at his return (vv. 20-23).[1] At Jesus' return, our perishable, dishonourable, weak, natural bodies (this is what our present bodies are like) will be raised as imperishable, glorious, powerful, spiritual bodies (this is what our resurrection bodies will be like; vv. 42-49). However, in the present we still exist in these perishable bodies.

But this is no reason for concern or disappointment, because we have been raised with Christ spiritually. The questions from Ephesians 2 point out that we were once dead in our sins (v. 1) but have now been made alive (resurrected) with Christ and raised up into heaven (vv. 5-6). This happened by the grace of God when we heard and believed the gospel message (vv. 8-9). The passage does not say anything explicitly about our physical bodies, other than that they are to be used for the good works that God has prepared for us to do.

The New Testament understands people as being made up of two parts: inner/outer, invisible/visible, or spiritual/physical. In accordance with this, the resurrection of Christians happens in two stages. First, when someone becomes a Christian the inner/invisible/spiritual part is resurrected (Eph 2:5-6). Second, when Jesus returns the outer/visible/physical part will be resurrected. The fact that the inner/invisible/spiritual part has already been resurrected guarantees that the outer/visible/physical part will be resurrected. And both of these resurrections are guaranteed to happen because Jesus was raised from the dead (1 Cor 15:20-23). This means that the Christian has already been resurrected in part in the present, and waits for the resurrection of the other part when Jesus returns.

 # To finish

These last questions draw together the points we have discovered and discussed in this study. The resurrection of the Christian occurs in two stages: the spiritual, when they believe the gospel by the grace of God, and the physical, at the return of Jesus. This means that we need no longer fear death because we know our future, thanks to the past, physical resurrection of Jesus. Further, we should have confidence of our situation before God in the present, because we have already been raised with Christ. Nothing can separate us from God—not even death!

---

1. 'Firstfruits' were the first part of the crop—grain, wine, animals—that were offered as a thanksgiving sacrifice to God as a representative of the total harvest that God had provided. You can read about it in Deuteronomy 26:1-11.

6. JESUS' RESURRECTION AND THE SPIRIT

▶ Remember 60/40/20

Getting started

The main point of this study is to teach people that the pouring out of the Spirit is one of the main consequences of Jesus' resurrection, and it marks the start of the new age: the resurrection age. We live in this new age because the risen Jesus raises us spiritually when he pours out his Spirit.

The opening question prompts people to consider the role and relationship of the Spirit to this timeline of resurrection, which is the question that this study seeks to answer.

Studying the passage

The two passages in this section make different points that contribute to the overall teaching aim of the study.

First, from Acts 2 it becomes evident that Jesus gives the Spirit to his people because God has physically raised him from the dead and made him the long-awaited Christ. So the questions help us to see that Jesus poured out the Spirit at Pentecost (v. 33) because, unlike David, Jesus' body did not see decay but was raised, demonstrating that he was God's promised king (vv. 30-31, 34). Because Jesus is the promised Christ, he is able to (and does) pour out the Spirit on his people (vv. 33, 36). That is, we know that Jesus is the Christ *because* God raised him from the dead and gave him the Spirit to pour out on his people. This is the main point of Peter's speech. You may also like to refer to Romans 1:4, where similar logic is evident in a shorter form. With the giving of the Spirit, the promised new age—the age of the resurrection and the Spirit—has started. This age was promised in the Old Testament, as seen from Peter's quoting of Joel 2:28-32 in Acts 2:16-21. The results of this new age are the gift of the Spirit to everyone who believes, and the forgiveness of sins (vv. 38-39). The forgiveness of sins is also explicitly noted as a result of the resurrection in 1 Corinthians 15:17, a passage to which you might like to refer in order to demonstrate the link elsewhere in the New Testament.

The second set of questions links the gift of the Spirit with personal salvation more closely. In a passage that is very similar to Ephesians 2:1-10 (which we read in the last study), Titus 3:3-8 speaks about our former way of life (v. 3) and about God saving us by rebirth and renewal of the Spirit, not because of our works but according to his mercy (v. 5). The gift of the Spirit makes us heirs of eternal life—guaranteeing that we will be physically raised when Jesus returns (v. 6) and resulting in our doing what is good (v. 8). That is, we are made members of the new resurrection age when we are given the Spirit—or, to put it differently, we are raised spiritually when the risen Jesus pours out his Spirit on us.

There is no need to feel concerned if there is some confusion over this concept, as we will return to it in the next study. For now, people should come away with the idea that the gift of the Spirit is the result of the resurrection of Jesus, and his pouring it out on us raises us spiritually to be his people.

 To finish

This question aims to summarize the main point of this study. Jesus now gives the Spirit to his people, and the Spirit raises them spiritually from death. This should result in us being people who are devoted to doing what is good. More explicit application is the focus of the next two studies.

7. LIVING THE RESURRECTED LIFE (I)

▶ Remember 60/40/20

 ## Getting started

The opening question to this study aims to move the focus from the resurrection itself to its implications in the life of the believer. The question asks about people's future hopes, expectations and dreams—because what we want in the future changes what we do in the present.

We have some knowledge of the guarantee of our future resurrection, so we need to let that shape what we do in the present. Further, we already have some of the benefits of the resurrection in the present (i.e. being spiritually raised), so we need to let that shape what we do, say and think.

Studying the passage

The first set of questions from Romans 8 focuses in on the relationship between the gift of the Spirit and its consequences for our lives in the present. The results of having the Spirit are that we are no longer controlled by the flesh but by the Spirit; that we belong to Jesus (v. 9); that we are no longer dead but alive (v. 10); and that the Spirit is giving life to our mortal bodies (v. 11). That is, the gift of the Spirit has raised us spiritually (summarizing the theme from the last two studies). Our spiritual resurrection has implications for the present: we must put to death sin and live as God's children. This new identity as God's children means that we are heirs. Our new identity is seen in our being like Jesus—suffering as he did for his obedience to God—so that we may also share in his glory when he returns. The Christian life is one that will be marked by suffering for doing good by obediently following God's design for life. The

Spirit gives us the desire and power to do this.

The second set of questions places all of this within the larger framework of the whole Bible and the physical resurrection. Our glory will be revealed when Jesus returns and brings all things to a conclusion. The history of the world has been building to this point—creation, fall, the death of Jesus for sin and his resurrection to life, and the gift of the Spirit—bringing in the last days and guaranteeing the final judgement and resurrection. We live in the last stage of God's unfolding plan, and as such we (and the whole creation) groan for the plan to be completed—for our glory to be revealed and our bodies to be redeemed. We have the Spirit, who is the firstfruits; the down payment; the guarantee of the physical resurrection and cosmic restoration.

 # To finish

The last section summarizes the study by two different means. First, the 'complete the quotes' section is meant to reinforce the main sequence of teaching and the main point. Our body is dead because of sin but our spirit is alive. We have been spiritually raised but we await the physical resurrection. So we are children of God, who are heirs and who call God 'Father' as we wait for the redemption of our bodies—the physical resurrection.

The consequence of this is that we are obliged to no longer live according to the flesh but according to the Spirit. So while we suffer in the present we should hope and dream for the day when our physical state will match our spiritual state—when we are given our new, glorious resurrected bodies.

8. LIVING THE RESURRECTED LIFE (II)

▶ **Remember 60/40/20**

 ## Getting started

This study aims to teach people about life in the Spirit in the present—the period in which we are spiritually (but not physically) raised. The opening question is meant to bring back to mind the teaching of the previous studies on the resurrection and its implications for our lives. Yet it opens up a possible confusion that needs correcting: that the Spirit-filled life is about signs, wonders and the miraculous. As we have seen, the Spirit unites us to Christ, which means present suffering but glorious future (Rom 8:17). The Spirit-filled life, then, is one of service of others, especially our Christian brothers and sisters.

Studying the passage

The theme of our outer/visible/physical bodies links the two passages from Romans. It is because Jesus was raised from death and now lives that we should consider ourselves dead to sin, not letting sin reign in our bodies (Rom 6:8-14). We saw in the last study that because we have the gift of the Spirit living in us (the Spirit of God who raised Jesus from the dead), we can be sure God will raise our bodies on the final day of judgement. Therefore, we live by the Spirit while we wait for the redemption of our bodies (Rom 8:9-14). (It might be worth revisiting this if people have forgotten, although the 'Getting started' question should have refreshed people's memories and gives you an easy point of reference.) Finally, it is because of the resurrection and the Spirit, summarized by Paul as 'the mercy of God' (Rom 12:1), that we should offer our bodies as living sacrifices to God. The resurrection of Jesus and the gift of the Spirit guarantee the resurrection of our bodies in the future, and so we should offer them to God in the present.

We then move on to think about some specific activities and ministries in which we should be involved. Paul uses the metaphor of a body to discuss the responsibilities that we have to each other at church (vv. 3-8) before moving on to outline our duty to all people (vv. 9-21). Spiritual resurrection and being controlled by the Spirit does not involve signs, wonders and the miraculous. Rather, it involves the service of others in love—something that is miraculous in its own right, but which we so often take for granted. Our spiritual act of worship is to follow the Spirit's lead in putting others and their interests before ourselves.

 ## To finish

The final section asks some particular application questions straight from the verses. These are best answered individually and then discussed in the group. Encourage people to be concrete in their thinking and in working through how they can/should change. If this is too direct, you could ask people to share with each other in pairs and pray together about their answers.

Feedback on this resource

We really appreciate getting feedback about our resources—not just suggestions for how to improve them, but also positive feedback and ways they can be used. We especially love to hear that the resources may have helped someone in their Christian growth.

You can send feedback to us via the 'Feedback' menu in our online store, or write to us at info@matthiasmedia.com.au.

Matthias Media is an evangelical publishing ministry that seeks to persuade all Christians of the truth of God's purposes in Jesus Christ as revealed in the Bible, and equip them with high-quality resources, so that by the work of the Holy Spirit they will:

- abandon their lives to the honour and service of Christ in daily holiness and decision-making
- pray constantly in Christ's name for the fruitfulness and growth of his gospel
- speak the Bible's life-changing word whenever and however they can—in the home, in the world and in the fellowship of his people.

Our resources range from Bible studies and books through to training courses, audio sermons and children's Sunday School material. To find out about more, and to access samples and free downloads, visit our website:

www.matthiasmedia.com

How to buy our resources

1. Direct from us over the internet:
   – in the US: www.matthiasmedia.com
   – in Australia: www.matthiasmedia.com.au

2. Direct from us by phone:
   – in the US: 1 866 407 4530
   – in Australia: 1300 051 220
   – international: +61 2 9233 4627

3. Through a range of outlets in various parts of the world. Visit **www.matthiasmedia.com/contact** for details about recommended retailers in your part of the world, including www.thegoodbook.co.uk in the United Kingdom.

4. Trade enquiries can be addressed to:
   – in the US and Canada: sales@matthiasmedia.com
   – in Australia and the rest of the world: sales@matthiasmedia.com.au

5. Visit **GoThereFor.com** for subscription-based access to a great-value range of digital resources.

> Register at our website for our **free** regular email update to receive information about the latest new resources, **exclusive special offers**, and free articles to help you grow in your Christian life and ministry.